By Rebecca Grabill

Illustrated by Isabella Grott

One Star, Three Kings

The Journey of Epiphany

PARACLETE PRESS
BREWSTER, MASSACHUSETTS

In the time of King Herod, after Jesus was born in Bethlehem of Judea, magi from the east came to Jerusalem, asking, "Where is the child who has been born king of the Jews? For we observed his star in the east and have come to pay him homage."

When King Herod heard this, he was frightened, and all Jerusalem with him, and calling together all the chief priests and scribes of the people, he inquired of them where the Messiah was to be born. They told him, "In Bethlehem of Judea, for so it has been written by the prophet:

> 'And you, Bethlehem, in the land of Judah,
> are by no means least among the rulers of Judah,
> for from you shall come a ruler
> who is to shepherd my people Israel.'"

Then Herod secretly called for the magi and learned from them the exact time when the star had appeared. Then he sent them to Bethlehem, saying, "Go and search diligently for the child, and when you have found him, bring me word so that I may also go and pay him homage."

When they had heard the king, they set out, and there, ahead of them, went the star that they had seen in the east, until it stopped over the place where the child was. When they saw that the star had stopped, they were overwhelmed with joy. On entering the house, they saw the child with Mary his mother, and they knelt down and paid him homage. Then, opening their treasure chests, they offered him gifts of gold, frankincense, and myrrh. And having been warned in a dream not to return to Herod, they left for their own country by another road.

—*Matthew 2:1–12*

The Kings

"Someday you will be king, Balthasar. And so I give you a star, only one." The king pointed to the sky.

"No one can give such a treasure as a star, Father," Balthasar replied.

"Oh, but I can," his father said, "for I am king."

The stars glistened overhead like scattered opals.

"How can I choose?"

"Seek your star, Balthasar, and you will find true treasure."

By day Balthasar worked alongside his people, gathering tears from the myrrh trees, as a good prince should, for no king is above the people's work.

By night he searched for a star he would call his own.

Season after season he grew, the trees grew, his knowledge of the sky grew, until he said, "Father, my star is not in this sky. I must go."

The old king nodded. "Seek and you will find it."

Waves rocked the boat as Balthasar balanced on the crowded deck.

“Do you hear that star?” a man beside him asked.

Balthasar asked in surprise, “How, Sir, can you *hear* a star?”

“I am no *Sir*, only Caspar.” Caspar laughed and raised his arms to the sky. “All the stars sing, but one of them sings especially to me.

“One star has been singing with a voice like my mother’s since I was but a boy. She called me away from my beautiful boswellia trees, singing of a kingdom far greater than my own.”

Balthasar strained his ears. Waves slapped wood. The boat’s sturdy frame creaked. “I wish I could hear this song, Sir.”

Caspar clapped a hand on Balthasar’s back. “Seek the star with me, young man, and we shall hear it together!”

Balthasar and Caspar continued over sea and land. They stopped at a grand palace as ancient as the desert sand around it.

“Good king, we seek a sign you may have seen,” Balthasar began.

Old King Melchior sighed. “I see very little, my sons.”

Caspar added eagerly, “Perhaps you’ve *heard* it, for our star sings!”

Melchior leaned forward. "A star? I have heard *of* a star. It is a thing of stories, tales told to me as a child." He closed his eyes. "Six hundred years …"

His voice trailed to silence.

Balthasar, with boldness of youth, said, "Please, tell us the story of this star."

Melchior reached for his staff. "Very well. It may be too late for me, but perhaps not for you."

I Wonder: Is the Story of the Magi True?

Read Matthew 2:1–12.

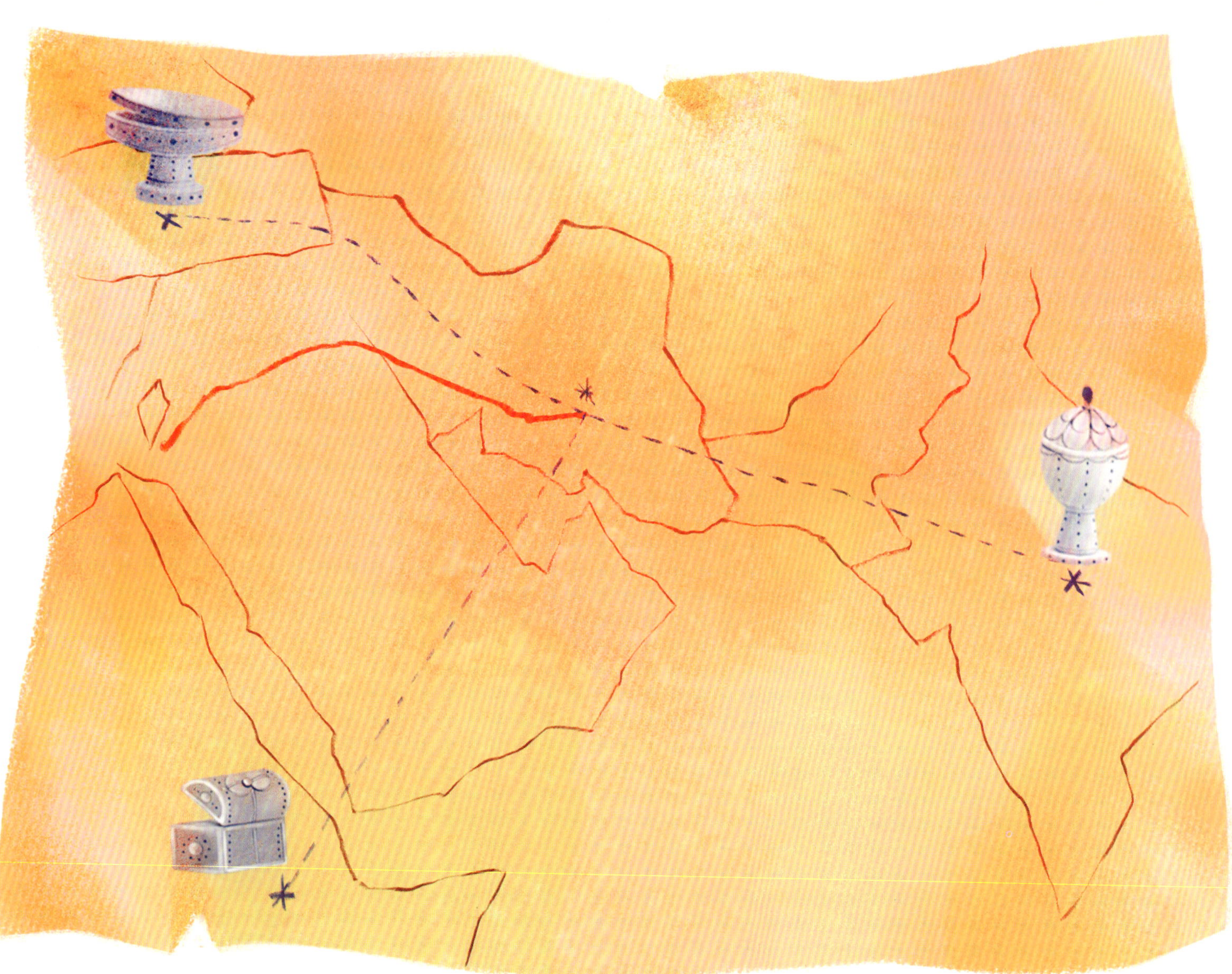

Fact or Fiction?

The Bible tells us very little about the Magi, but what it does tell us, we know to be true. That part of the story is fact. In this book, much of our story—the Magi's personalities and lives before they found baby Jesus, what they said, their childhood dreams or emotions—comes from imagination deepened by historical research. Some details, however, came not from the Bible or imagination, but were passed down over time.

Legend & Tradition

For a story more than two thousand years old, like this one about the Magi, legend and tradition overlap. Tradition sets the Magi's number at three and gives us their names, although some stories provide different names than the ones used here. For example, in Ethiopia, Caspar's name was recorded as Hor, Balthasar's name as Basanater, and Melchior's name as Karsudan. According to early writers, each of the Magi came from a different part of the ancient world. Balthasar came from southern Arabia or Ethiopia, Caspar from India, and Melchior from Persia, a kingdom which spanned much of northern Arabia and included modern-day Iran and parts of nearby countries such as Iraq, Turkey, and Syria.

The Prophecy

"This place is as old as time," Melchior said. "After the great flood, people built a tower that reached to the stars. This is what remains."

Shadows from the crumbling ruins fell like teeth across the sand.

"It hardly reaches the stars," Caspar said.

"They never finished it." Melchior climbed, his feet sure even with dim sight. "The peoples scattered to distant lands."

"To my land of myrrh trees, and to Caspar's land of boswellia," Balthasar said.

Melchior nodded. "The people scattered to all corners of the map, and now you return from those corners, to the beginning." He squinted at the darkening sky. "Come, climb. It is time. Perhaps you will see what I have long been seeking."

A desert breeze cooled their faces as the younger Magi helped Melchior up the tower's narrow stairs.

"Almost six hundred years ago, the great prophet Daniel walked this very ground," Melchior explained. "Daniel prophesied of a King, one for all peoples of the earth." Melchior stopped where the wall opened to the night sky. "Daniel told us *when* to look for this King … and the time is near."

Then Melchior spoke the words of wisdom past, "A star shall come out of Jacob, a bright light to draw all nations."*

The sky stretched above them. Stars flickered to life one by one, their lights glistening in Melchior's eyes.

Caspar listened to the silence.

Balthasar whispered the words of his father, "Seek your star, and you will find true treasure."

* From Numbers 24:17 and Tobit 13:11.

"Listen!" Caspar leapt to his feet. "That star, there! Do you hear it?"

One star glowed in a way Balthasar had never before seen. "I see … my star."

"Tell me what you see, what you hear," Melchior leaned on his staff.

"It's more brilliant than treasure," Balthasar said.

Caspar closed his eyes. "I hear a woman's voice singing a song of joy! She is the Lord's servant, yet she will be the mother of a King."

Melchior took Balthasar's hand, then Caspar's. "The star will lead us to the promised King!"

I Wonder: When Did the Magi First See the Star?

Read Genesis 12:3 and Luke 3:6.

An Angel for the Ages

Many scholars believe the star that led the Magi to Jesus appeared at the time of the Annunciation, when the angel Gabriel announced that Mary would bear God's Son (recorded in Matthew).

Did you know that the angel Gabriel is mentioned only three other times in the Bible? Gabriel delivered similar news of a coming baby to Zechariah the priest. And Gabriel made two visits to Daniel nearly six hundred years before.

Daniel was a prophet and a captive in Babylon. Gabriel's visits helped explain Daniel's prophecies about a King of all kings who would bring an everlasting kingdom. If the Magi knew of Daniel's prophecy, they would know that the time foretold of this everlasting King had come!

Where Did the Magi Come From?

In the story of the Tower of Babel, people tried to build a tower to God, but God confused their languages and scattered them. After Babel, God's first covenant (a binding promise) of blessing and salvation was given to one person, Abraham. It was given to one person, but this promise was for all people. In the Old Testament, we're promised more than 58 times that all people will be blessed! In the New Testament, John the Baptist says again how the Messiah comes for all mankind.

According to many stories, the Magi came from every corner of the map as drawn at that point in history. The Magi represent all nations bowing before Jesus Christ.

Workers shouted as they loaded camels with supplies for the journey.

Balthasar considered the treasures he had brought from home: opals, pearls, figures of carved ivory. What gift could he bring to the King of all kings?

His father's words played in his memory like gentle music. "Seek and you will find true treasure."

The Star

Only one item was fit for such a King. Yet it seemed too small.

Small, but priceless.

Balthasar tucked it, carefully wrapped, in his camel's pack.

Caspar called from the gate, "The star is moving! We must ride!"

Night after night they traveled, and night after night Caspar listened. The song changed—at times a peaceful melody, at others a faithful prayer.

Tonight, the singer sang with joy, *The Almighty has done great things for me, and holy is his name!*

Tears flowed freely down Caspar's wind-chapped cheeks. He no longer tried to wipe them away.

He inhaled sweetness more lovely than the fragrant gift he carried.

The sweet scent was like the song of the mother of this King, carried through the miles on the wings of a desert breeze.

On every clear night for months Melchior asked the same question: "What does it look like, the star?"

His vision was dim, but his imagination painted the picture. He saw the star as a flame, its light blazing across the sand like the pillar of fire from stories of old.

Long before Daniel, the Hebrew people escaped slavery and traveled across the desert to a land of promise. A light of God's making led the way.

Was this trip any different? Melchior wondered.

They followed this light all the way to Jerusalem. Tomorrow they would greet the king of the land.

Tonight, however, clouds hid the star. Melchior could only wait and imagine.

While Caspar and Melchior met with the famed King Herod, Balthasar paced.

Clouds blanketed the dark sky, as they had for days. “My beautiful Star, where are you?”

A breeze lifted Balthasar’s cloak, tossing it around him. The clouds tossed too, shifting to reveal a tiny spark of light.

Balthasar quickly lifted his astrolabe. He measured, caught his breath.

Yes, his star had at last returned, and it was moving!

A commotion of voices and torchlight broke the silence. Caspar crossed the paving stones in running steps. Melchior hurried behind him.

"To Bethlehem!" Caspar shouted; his smile as wide as the sky. "We must ride to Bethlehem!"

Without waiting for servants or guards, the three mounted their camels.
They rode from Herod's palace with the speed of the wind.

I Wonder: What Did the Magi Really Follow?

Read Numbers 24:17 and Tobit 13:11.

Star of Wonder

We have wondered for centuries, what was the Magi's star?

Supernova (star explosion): Some ancient artwork shows a bright star, but no historians wrote about it, so most experts don't think the Magi's star was a supernova.

Comet: We know where and when comets would have passed through the night sky in ages past. Between what we know and what ancient historians recorded, the star was probably not a comet.

Conjunction: Some modern astronomers suggest that the star was actually a movement of planets so small that only those looking would see it. Detailed computer models show unusual conjunctions around the time of Jesus's birth—planets appearing so close together that they seem like a single star. Could one of these conjunctions have been the star?

Supernatural light: Some experts don't think the star was a star at all but was some other form of heavenly light.

The actual star that guided the Magi is a mystery to this day.

The Gifts

"There!" Balthasar pointed toward the flicker of starlight. "It has stopped."

As he spoke, the last of the clouds parted and thinned. In mere moments, the night grew brilliantly clear.

One star shone brighter than the rest, the village of Bethlehem silent beneath it.

Caspar tilted his head, listening.

A soft, sweet melody drifted through the night from somewhere in the huddle of homes. They could all hear it.

Melchior blinked, his vision clearing like the sky overhead. "I see something … a light, glowing there." He gripped Balthasar's hand. "Tell me it is not mere imagination. Tell me I see the Bright Morning Star."

Melchior paused in the doorway of the small house.

A young woman, Mary, welcomed him inside, surprise and wonder in her gaze. A child peered out from behind her skirt.

Melchior blinked in the brightness.

“The star,” he whispered, sinking to his knees. “The King of kings.”

He glanced at the gift in his hand. “I have brought too little. All the gold in my treasury, every jewel from every crown in all of Persia …” He placed the chest of gold before the child. “Even that would not be enough.”

Caspar carried his gift, as fragrant as prayers lifting to heaven.

"Lady," Caspar said, tears on his cheeks. "I heard your song."

She took his hand, and with a grace that surpassed that of any queen, led him into the house.

Caspar knelt beside Melchior as Mary placed his hand in her child's.

The fragrance of Caspar's gift filled the room, but the true gift stood before them. Though he was just a child, he was also King and God; he gazed on Caspar with attention and love.

The child's love grew like the aroma of frankincense, like swirling smoke wrapping them all in its sweetness. Caspar had never felt such love before.

Balthasar carried his gift in trembling hands.

Already, Melchior's gold spilled out of the chest and across the small home's floor. Caspar's frankincense tinged the air with sweetness.

Balthasar bowed to the earth and offered his gift. "The purest of myrrh—the tears of my people," he said. "It is for weddings and … for burials."

A soft gasp broke the silence. Mary pressed a hand to her heart as Joseph wrapped his arm around her shoulder.

Balthasar saw a vision—the child grown into a man. His broken heart aflame and glistening, rubies spilling from it, filling a cup with the greatest treasure of all time, God's pure gift—a sacrifice.

I Wonder: Why Did the Magi Bring Gifts?

Read Song of Solomon 3:6 and John 19:39.

Gold: Gold was so beautiful, rare, and valuable that it took 13 silver coins to equal one gold coin in ancient Rome. All the items in the temple were overlaid with gold, showing God's Kingship over all the earth. Gold was a gift for a King!

Frankincense: Ancient Rome imported three thousand tons of frankincense a year. Why? To cover the odors of the city's open sewers. In the temple, frankincense not only gave a beautiful aroma when burned on the Altar of Incense, but it also represented the prayers of the people. It was part of the annual sacrifice offered by the High Priest to atone for Israel's sins. A gift of frankincense showed Jesus was King but also High Priest, able to lift our prayers, and our sins.

Myrrh: Myrrh was a gift of prophecy, even in how it was harvested. Harvesters sliced the myrrh tree's bark and waited for the sticky sap that flowed from the wound to harden into dark, reddish colored tears of resin. These they collected and made into oil.

Would you believe that this oil used to embalm the dead, made from wounded trees, was also called the *oil of joy*. Esther bathed in myrrh oil as part of her preparation to meet the king, and myrrh is mentioned in Song of Solomon, a love song between the bridegroom and his beloved. Myrrh, a surprising, yet beautiful gift, whispers the future story: Jesus, yet a child, will be wounded like the myrrh tree. He will be killed, his body dressed with myrrh. But in rising from the dead, he will invite us to celebrate forever the great wedding banquet!

The Celebration

The roads home seemed far shorter than the roads they traveled to find their King. Soon, Balthasar's myrrh trees appeared on the horizon.

His father met him on the road. "Did you find your star, Son?"

"I found nothing for myself," Balthasar said. "I cannot keep this joy for myself any more than I can own a star. The gift is for all!"

His father smiled. "You have indeed found treasure greater than any that was or is or ever shall be."

The truth of his father's words stayed with Balthasar through the years. He asked every visiting merchant if they'd heard of the great King who held the tears of the people. No one had … until a man shared the good news of a healer and prophet in Jerusalem.

Balthasar set out to find him that very day.

Far away in India, all the stars had returned to their usual places, but Caspar continued to listen. On quiet nights, he still heard a singer's pure, sweet voice, the voice of the Holy Mother.

Over the years, she sang with happiness, with stillness, with contentment and joy.

Until one night, her voice cracked in agony, and her song turned to weeping.

Though it was night, Caspar rose. He needed to find his King.

Melchior, aged and frail, also thought of the King of kings. He longed to look upon his King one last time.

And so, he, with the others, returned to Jerusalem.

Instead of their King, they found … stories.

They found stories of their King's baptism, stories of his miraculous changing of water into wine.

They found stories of healings and forgiveness. They found a story of a love so great that their King poured out his life so all the people of the world would one day never shed tears again.

And they believed.

Thomas baptized them, and the Magi shared their Good News of great joy with everyone who had ears to listen.

Through his sharing, Melchior at last found the one gift worth more than gold, more than every jewel from every crown in all his kingdom. He found the one gift worthy of his King and God.

Melchior and Caspar and Balthasar gave Jesus their lives.*

* Balthasar, Caspar, and Melchior are martyrs and saints, celebrated on January 6, Epiphany!

I Wonder: How Is Epiphany Celebrated Today?

In the celebration of Epiphany, in some countries called Three Kings' Day, all people in every corner of the world celebrate the coming of God in human form. More than 1700 years ago the church began to celebrate, and we celebrate still, in different ways in different places.

In Italy, children follow a procession of people dressed as Magi carrying gifts. Sometimes even camels are part of the procession!

In Poland and Central Europe, families write a blessing over their front doors with chalk. The letters CMB stand for the names of the Magi, and for the Latin phrase *Christus mansionem benedicat* (may Christ bless the house).

I Wonder: When Did the Magi First See the Star?

Read Genesis 12:3 and Luke 3:6.

An Angel for the Ages

Many scholars believe the star that led the Magi to Jesus appeared at the time of the Annunciation, when the angel Gabriel announced that Mary would bear God's Son (recorded in Matthew).

Did you know that the angel Gabriel is mentioned only three other times in the Bible? Gabriel delivered similar news of a coming baby to Zechariah the priest. And Gabriel made two visits to Daniel nearly six hundred years before.

Daniel was a prophet and a captive in Babylon. Gabriel's visits helped explain Daniel's prophecies about a King of all kings who would bring an everlasting kingdom. If the Magi knew of Daniel's prophecy, they would know that the time foretold of this everlasting King had come!